# HAL•LEONARD

# JAZZ PLAY-ALONG®

Book and CD for B♭, E♭, C and Bass Clef Instruments

# MODAL JAZZ

**VOLUME 179**

Arranged and Produced
by Mark Taylor

## BOOK

| TITLE | C Treble Instruments | PAGE NUMBERS | | |
|---|---|---|---|---|
| | | B♭ Instruments | E♭ Instruments | C Bass Instruments |
| Black Narcissus | 4 | 18 | 32 | 46 |
| Bolivia | 6 | 20 | 34 | 48 |
| Cantelope | 5 | 19 | 33 | 47 |
| Caravan | 8 | 22 | 36 | 50 |
| Contemplation | 10 | 24 | 38 | 52 |
| Freedom Jazz Dance | 11 | 25 | 39 | 53 |
| Impressions | 12 | 26 | 40 | 54 |
| Shutterbug | 13 | 27 | 41 | 55 |
| So What | 14 | 28 | 42 | 56 |
| Yes or No | 16 | 30 | 44 | 58 |

## CD

| TITLE | CD Track Number Split Track/Melody | CD Track Number Full Stereo Track |
|---|---|---|
| Black Narcissus | 1 | 2 |
| Bolivia | 3 | 4 |
| Cantelope Island | 5 | 6 |
| Caravan | 7 | 8 |
| Contemplation | 9 | 10 |
| Freedom Jazz Dance | 11 | 12 |
| Impressions | 13 | 14 |
| Shutterbug | 15 | 16 |
| So What | 17 | 18 |
| Yes or No | 19 | 20 |
| B♭ Tuning Notes | | 21 |

One Man Band, Guitar and Squeeze-Box, 1951 (oil on board), Banting, John (1902-72)
Private Collection / Photo © Agnew's, London / Bridgeman Images

ISBN 978-1-4803-5489-0

# HAL•LEONARD®
## CORPORATION

7777 W. BLUEMOUND RD. P.O. BOX 13819 MILWAUKEE, WI 53213

For all works contained herein:
Unauthorized copying, arranging, adapting, recording, Internet posting, public performance,
or other distribution of the printed or recorded music in this publication is an infringement of copyright.
Infringers are liable under the law.

Visit Hal Leonard Online at
**www.halleonard.com**

# MODAL JAZZ

## Volume 179

## Arranged and Produced
## by Mark Taylor

**Featured Players:**

Graham Breedlove–Trumpet
John Desalme–Sax
Tony Nalker–Piano
Paul Henry–Bass
Todd Harrison–Drums
Steve Fidyk–Drums

**Recorded at Bias Studios, Springfield, Virginia
Bob Dawson, Engineer**

## HOW TO USE THE CD:

Each song has <u>two</u> tracks:

### 1) Split Track/Melody

**Woodwind, Brass, Keyboard,** and **Mallet Players** can use this track as a learning tool for melody style and inflection.

**Bass Players** can learn and perform with this track – remove the recorded bass track by turning down the volume on the LEFT channel.

**Keyboard** and **Guitar Players** can learn and perform with this track – remove the recorded piano part by turning down the volume on the RIGHT channel.

### 2) Full Stereo Track

**Soloists** or **Groups** can learn and perform with this accompaniment track with the RHYTHM SECTION only.

# BLACK NARCISSUS

BY JOE HENDERSON

Copyright © 1969 Johen Music
Copyright Renewed
This arrangement Copyright © 2015 Johen Music
International Copyright Secured   All Rights Reserved

# CANTELOPE ISLAND

BY HERBIE HANCOCK

**CD**
◆ **5** : SPLIT TRACK/MELODY
◆ **6** : FULL STEREO TRACK

**C VERSION**

Copyright © 1964 (Renewed) by Hancock Music (BMI)
This arrangement Copyright © 2015 by Hancock Music
International Copyright Secured   All Rights Reserved

# BOLIVIA

BY CEDAR WALTON

**CD**

◆3 : SPLIT TRACK/MELODY

◆4 : FULL STEREO TRACK

C VERSION

Copyright © 1975 (Renewed 2003) Vernita Music
This arrangement Copyright © 2015 Vernita Music
All Rights Reserved   Used by Permission

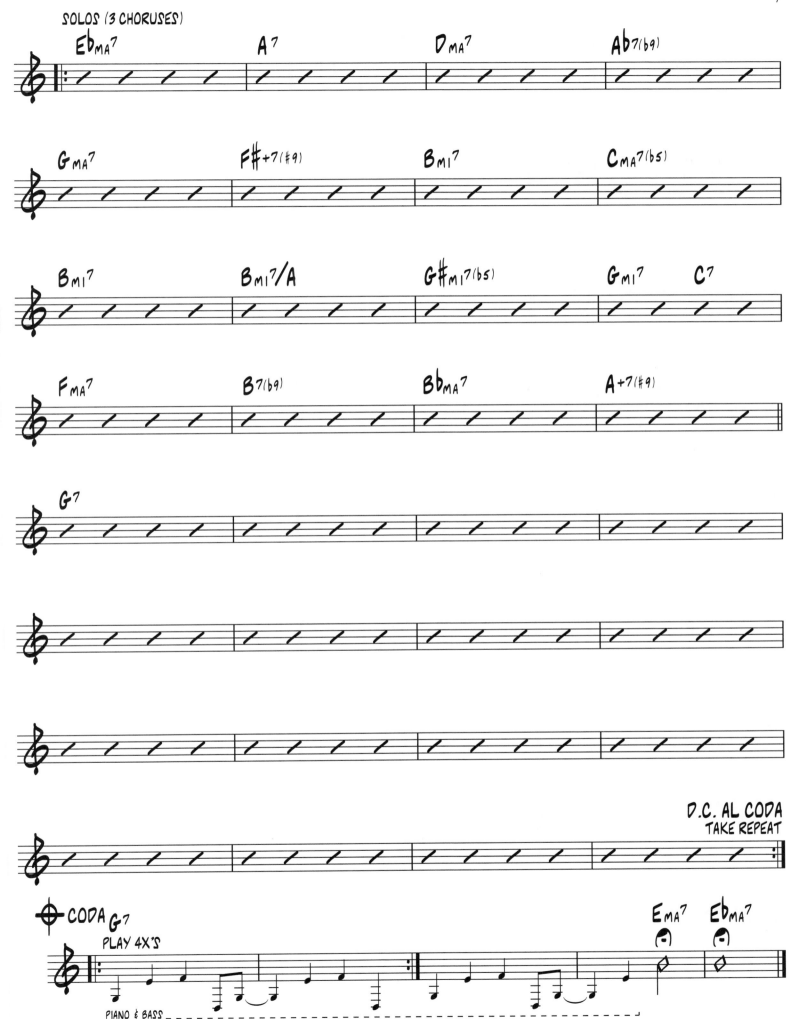

# CARAVAN

WORDS AND MUSIC BY DUKE ELLINGTON, IRVING MILLS AND JUAN TIZOL

C VERSION

Copyright © 1937 Sony/ATV Music Publishing LLC and EMI Mills Music Inc. in the U.S.A.
Copyright Renewed
This arrangement Copyright © 2015 Sony/ATV Music Publishing LLC and EMI Mills Music Inc. in the U.S.A.
All Rights on behalf of Sony/ATV Music Publishing LLC Administered by Sony/ATV Music Publishing LLC, 424 Church Street, Suite 1200, Nashville, TN 37219
All Rights for the world outside the U.S.A. Administered by EMI Mills Music Inc. (Publishing) and Alfred Music (Print)
International Copyright Secured   All Rights Reserved

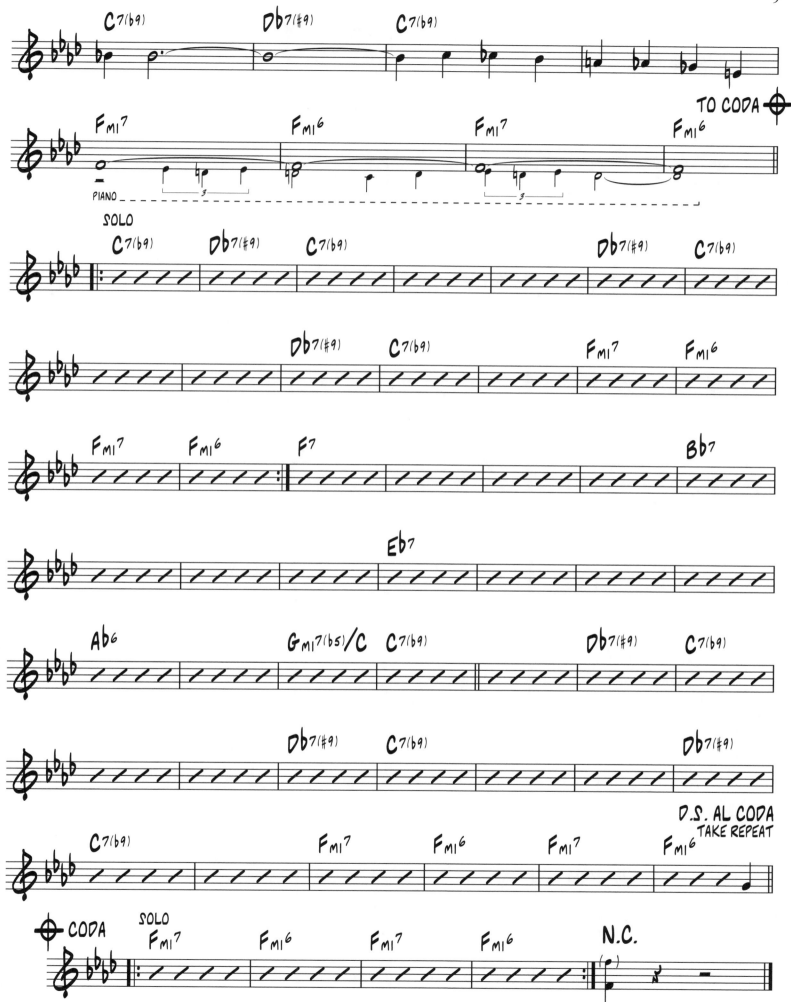

# CONTEMPLATION

**9** : SPLIT TRACK/MELODY
**10** : FULL STEREO TRACK

C VERSION

BY McCoy Tyner

Copyright © 1963 Aisha Music
Copyright Renewed
This arrangement Copyright © 2015 Aisha Music
Administered by Prestige Music
International Copyright Secured   All Rights Reserved

# FREEDOM JAZZ DANCE

BY EDDIE HARRIS

CD
- 11 : SPLIT TRACK/MELODY
- 12 : FULL STEREO TRACK

C VERSION

Copyright © 1965 Seventh House Ltd.
Copyright Renewed
This arrangement Copyright © 2015 Seventh House Ltd.
All Rights Reserved    Used by Permission

CD
13 : SPLIT TRACK/MELODY
14 : FULL STEREO TRACK

# IMPRESSIONS

BY JOHN COLTRANE

C VERSION

Copyright © 1974 (Renewed) JOWCOL MUSIC LLC
This arrangement Copyright © 2015 JOWCOL MUSIC LLC
International Copyright Secured   All Rights Reserved

# SHUTTERBUG

BY J.J. JOHNSON

CD
15 : SPLIT TRACK/MELODY
16 : FULL STEREO TRACK

C VERSION

Copyright © 1960 TWO JAYS PUBLISHING CO.
Copyright Renewed
This arrangement Copyright © 2015 TWO JAYS PUBLISHING CO.
International Copyright Secured   All Rights Reserved

# SO WHAT

BY MILES DAVIS

**CD**

🔷**17** : SPLIT TRACK/MELODY
🔷**18** : FULL STEREO TRACK

**C VERSION**

Copyright © 1959 Jazz Horn Music Corporation
Copyright Renewed
This arrangement Copyright © 2002 Jazz Horn Music Corporation
All Rights Administered by Songs Of Kobalt Music Publishing
All Rights Reserved   Used by Permission

# YES OR NO

BY WAYNE SHORTER

C VERSION

Copyright © 1964 Miyako Music
Copyright Renewed
This arrangement Copyright © 2015 Miyako Music
All Rights Administered by Songs Of Kobalt Music Publishing
All Rights Reserved   Used by Permission

# BLACK NARCISSUS

BY JOE HENDERSON

Copyright © 1969 Johen Music
Copyright Renewed
This arrangement Copyright © 2015 Johen Music
International Copyright Secured   All Rights Reserved

# CANTELOPE ISLAND

BY HERBIE HANCOCK

**CD**
5 : SPLIT TRACK/MELODY
6 : FULL STEREO TRACK

**Bb VERSION**

Copyright © 1964 (Renewed) by Hancock Music (BMI)
This arrangement Copyright © 2015 by Hancock Music
International Copyright Secured   All Rights Reserved

# BOLIVIA

BY CEDAR WALTON

Copyright © 1975 (Renewed 2003) Vernita Music
This arrangement Copyright © 2015 Vernita Music
All Rights Reserved   Used by Permission

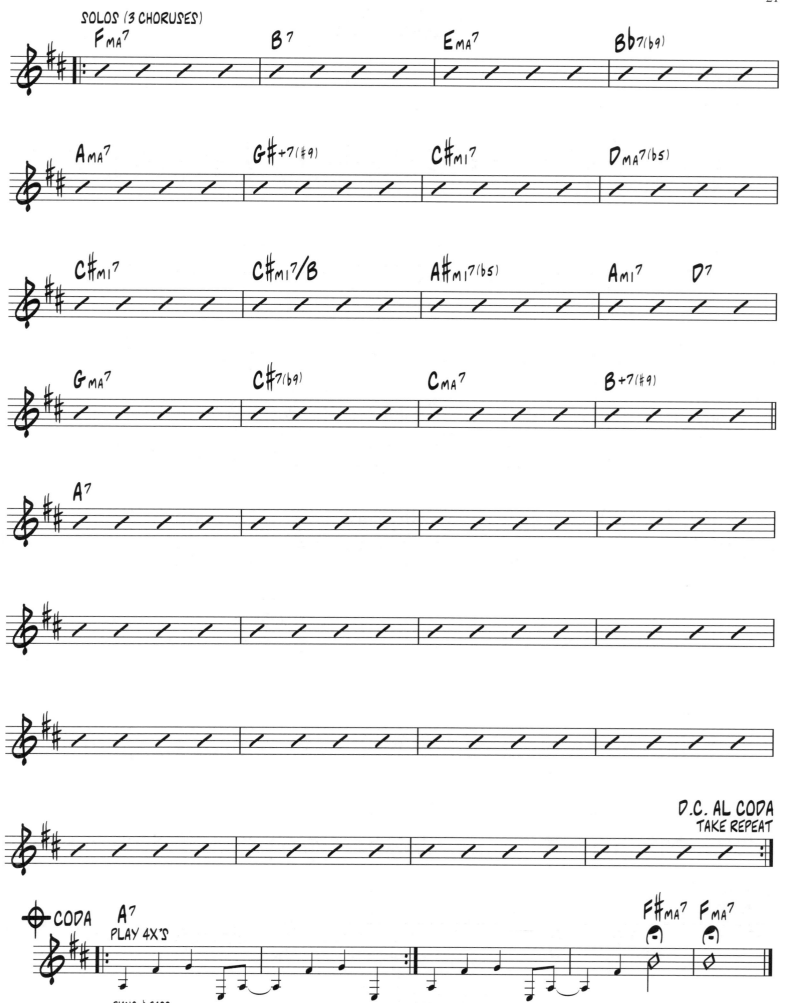

CD
**7** : SPLIT TRACK/MELODY
**8** : FULL STEREO TRACK

# CARAVAN

WORDS AND MUSIC BY DUKE ELLINGTON,
IRVING MILLS AND JUAN TIZOL

**Bb VERSION**

Copyright © 1937 Sony/ATV Music Publishing LLC and EMI Mills Music Inc. in the U.S.A.
Copyright Renewed
This arrangement Copyright © 2015 Sony/ATV Music Publishing LLC and EMI Mills Music Inc. in the U.S.A.
All Rights on behalf of Sony/ATV Music Publishing LLC Administered by Sony/ATV Music Publishing LLC, 424 Church Street, Suite 1200, Nashville, TN 37219
All Rights for the world outside the U.S.A. Administered by EMI Mills Music Inc. (Publishing) and Alfred Music (Print)
International Copyright Secured   All Rights Reserved

# CONTEMPLATION

CD

◆9: SPLIT TRACK/MELODY

◆10: FULL STEREO TRACK

Bb VERSION

BY McCOY TYNER

Copyright © 1963 Aisha Music
Copyright Renewed
This arrangement Copyright © 2015 Aisha Music
Administered by Prestige Music
International Copyright Secured   All Rights Reserved

**CD**
- 11: SPLIT TRACK/MELODY
- 12: FULL STEREO TRACK

# FREEDOM JAZZ DANCE

BY EDDIE HARRIS

**Bb VERSION**

MEDIUM SECOND LINE FUNK

N.C.

mf

C7(#9)

PIANO

N.C.

C7(#9)

PIANO

N.C.

C7(#9)

3

SOLOS (PLAY 16X'S)

N.C.

C7(#9)

1ST X ONLY

N.C.

C7(#9)

N.C.

LAST X ONLY

PIANO

C7(#9)

N.C.

PIANO

Bbsus/C   Bsus/C#   Csus/D   C#sus/D#   Dsus/E   Ebsus/F   Esus/F#   Fsus/G   C7(#9)

3

1.

2.

Copyright © 1965 Seventh House Ltd.
Copyright Renewed
This arrangement Copyright © 2015 Seventh House Ltd.
All Rights Reserved   Used by Permission

# IMPRESSIONS

BY JOHN COLTRANE

Bb VERSION

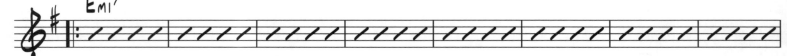

Copyright © 1974 (Renewed) JOWCOL MUSIC LLC
This arrangement Copyright © 2015 JOWCOL MUSIC LLC
International Copyright Secured   All Rights Reserved

# SHUTTERBUG

BY J.J. JOHNSON

CD
◆15 : SPLIT TRACK/MELODY
◆16 : FULL STEREO TRACK

**Bb VERSION**

Copyright © 1960 TWO JAYS PUBLISHING CO.
Copyright Renewed
This arrangement Copyright © 2015 TWO JAYS PUBLISHING CO.
International Copyright Secured   All Rights Reserved

# SO WHAT

BY MILES DAVIS

Bb VERSION

Copyright © 1959 Jazz Horn Music Corporation
Copyright Renewed
This arrangement Copyright © 2002 Jazz Horn Music Corporation
All Rights Administered by Songs Of Kobalt Music Publishing
All Rights Reserved   Used by Permission

# YES OR NO

CD
⟨19⟩ : SPLIT TRACK/MELODY
⟨20⟩ : FULL STEREO TRACK

BY WAYNE SHORTER

**Bb VERSION**

Copyright © 1964 Miyako Music
Copyright Renewed
This arrangement Copyright © 2015 Miyako Music
All Rights Administered by Songs Of Kobalt Music Publishing
All Rights Reserved   Used by Permission

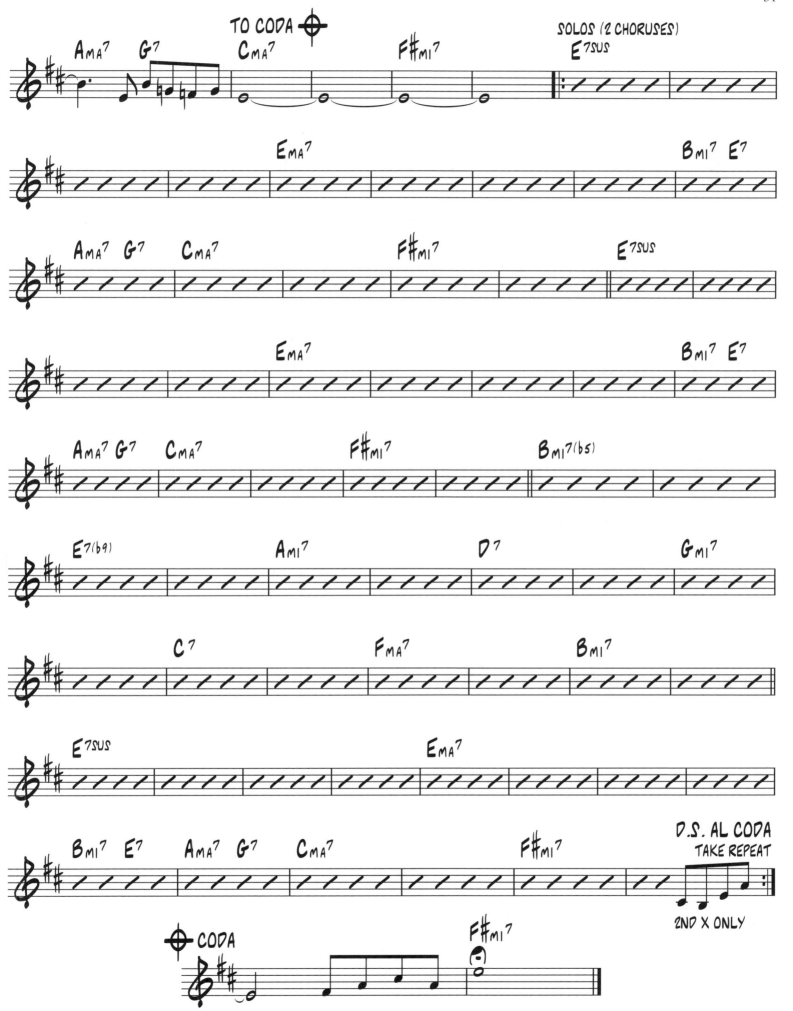

CD
1 : SPLIT TRACK/MELODY
2 : FULL STEREO TRACK

# BLACK NARCISSUS

BY JOE HENDERSON

Eb VERSION

Copyright © 1969 Johen Music
Copyright Renewed
This arrangement Copyright © 2015 Johen Music
International Copyright Secured   All Rights Reserved

CD
5 : SPLIT TRACK/MELODY
6 : FULL STEREO TRACK

# CANTELOPE ISLAND

BY HERBIE HANCOCK

Eb VERSION

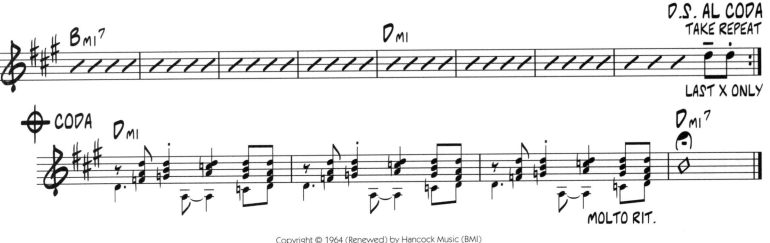

Copyright © 1964 (Renewed) by Hancock Music (BMI)
This arrangement Copyright © 2015 by Hancock Music
International Copyright Secured   All Rights Reserved

# BOLIVIA

BY CEDAR WALTON

Eb VERSION

Copyright © 1975 (Renewed 2003) Vernita Music
This arrangement Copyright © 2015 Vernita Music
All Rights Reserved   Used by Permission

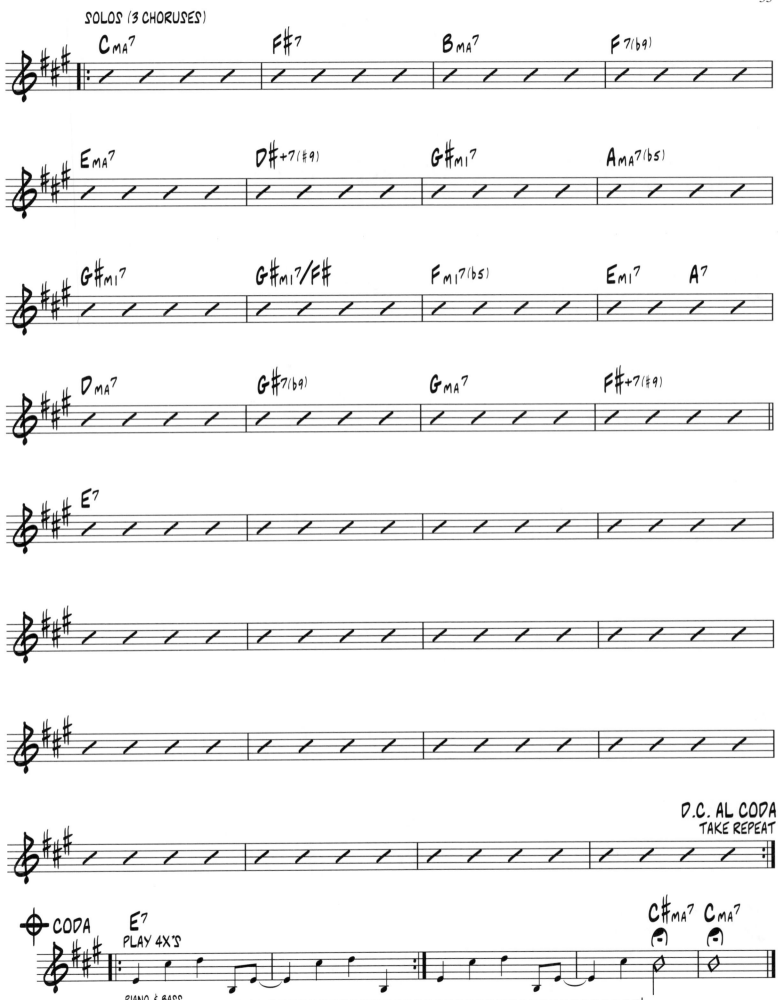

# CARAVAN

WORDS AND MUSIC BY DUKE ELLINGTON,
IRVING MILLS AND JUAN TIZOL

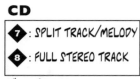

Copyright © 1937 Sony/ATV Music Publishing LLC and EMI Mills Music Inc. in the U.S.A.
Copyright Renewed
This arrangement Copyright © 2015 Sony/ATV Music Publishing LLC and EMI Mills Music Inc. in the U.S.A.
All Rights on behalf of Sony/ATV Music Publishing LLC Administered by Sony/ATV Music Publishing LLC, 424 Church Street, Suite 1200, Nashville, TN 37219
All Rights for the world outside the U.S.A. Administered by EMI Mills Music Inc. (Publishing) and Alfred Music (Print)
International Copyright Secured   All Rights Reserved

# CONTEMPLATION

BY McCOY TYNER

Copyright © 1963 Aisha Music
Copyright Renewed
This arrangement Copyright © 2015 Aisha Music
Administered by Prestige Music
International Copyright Secured   All Rights Reserved

# FREEDOM JAZZ DANCE

BY EDDIE HARRIS

**CD**
**11** : SPLIT TRACK/MELODY
**12** : FULL STEREO TRACK

Eb VERSION

Copyright © 1965 Seventh House Ltd.
Copyright Renewed
This arrangement Copyright © 2015 Seventh House Ltd.
All Rights Reserved   Used by Permission

# IMPRESSIONS

BY JOHN COLTRANE

Eb VERSION

Copyright © 1974 (Renewed) JOWCOL MUSIC LLC
This arrangement Copyright © 2015 JOWCOL MUSIC LLC
International Copyright Secured  All Rights Reserved

# SHUTTERBUG

BY J.J. JOHNSON

CD
15 : SPLIT TRACK/MELODY
16 : FULL STEREO TRACK

Eb VERSION

Copyright © 1960 TWO JAYS PUBLISHING CO.
Copyright Renewed
This arrangement Copyright © 2015 TWO JAYS PUBLISHING CO.
International Copyright Secured   All Rights Reserved

# SO WHAT

CD
17 : SPLIT TRACK/MELODY
18 : FULL STEREO TRACK

BY MILES DAVIS

Eb VERSION

Copyright © 1959 Jazz Horn Music Corporation
Copyright Renewed
This arrangement Copyright © 2002 Jazz Horn Music Corporation
All Rights Administered by Songs Of Kobalt Music Publishing
All Rights Reserved   Used by Permission

# YES OR NO

BY WAYNE SHORTER

Eb VERSION

Copyright © 1964 Miyako Music
Copyright Renewed
This arrangement Copyright © 2015 Miyako Music
All Rights Administered by Songs Of Kobalt Music Publishing
All Rights Reserved   Used by Permission

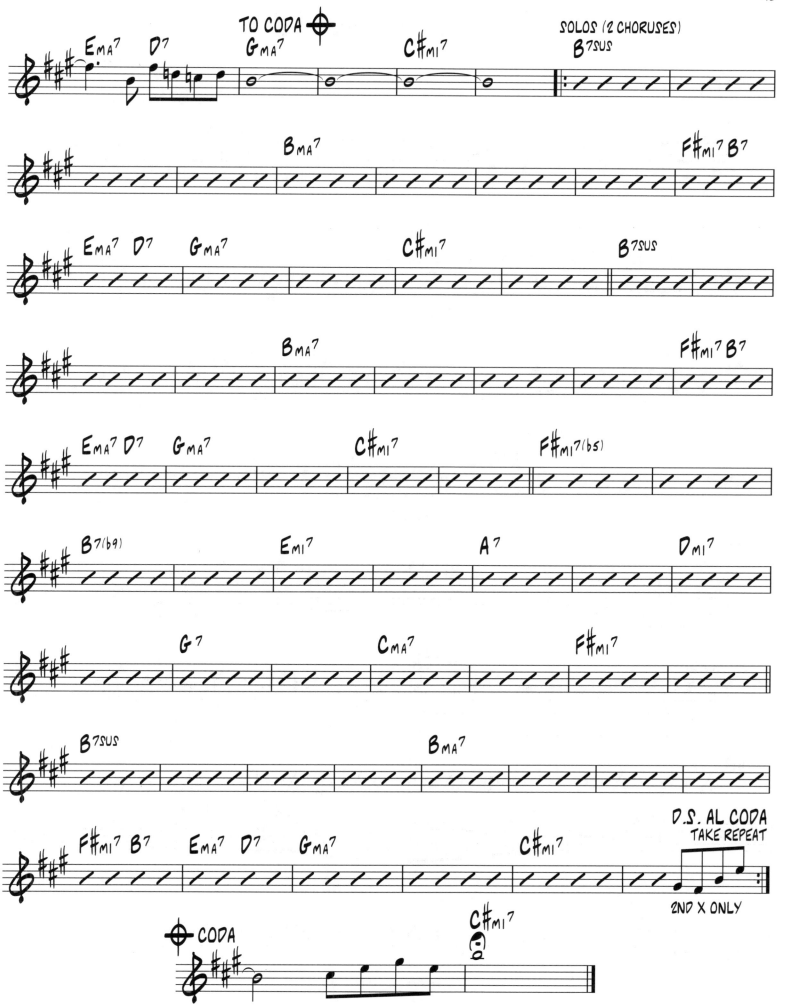

# BLACK NARCISSUS

BY JOE HENDERSON

Copyright © 1969 Johen Music
Copyright Renewed
This arrangement Copyright © 2015 Johen Music
International Copyright Secured   All Rights Reserved

# CANTELOPE ISLAND

By Herbie Hancock

Copyright © 1964 (Renewed) by Hancock Music (BMI)
This arrangement Copyright © 2015 by Hancock Music
International Copyright Secured   All Rights Reserved

# BOLIVIA

BY CEDAR WALTON

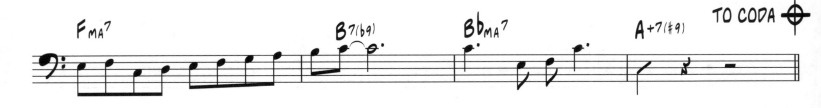

Copyright © 1975 (Renewed 2003) Vernita Music
This arrangement Copyright © 2015 Vernita Music
All Rights Reserved   Used by Permission

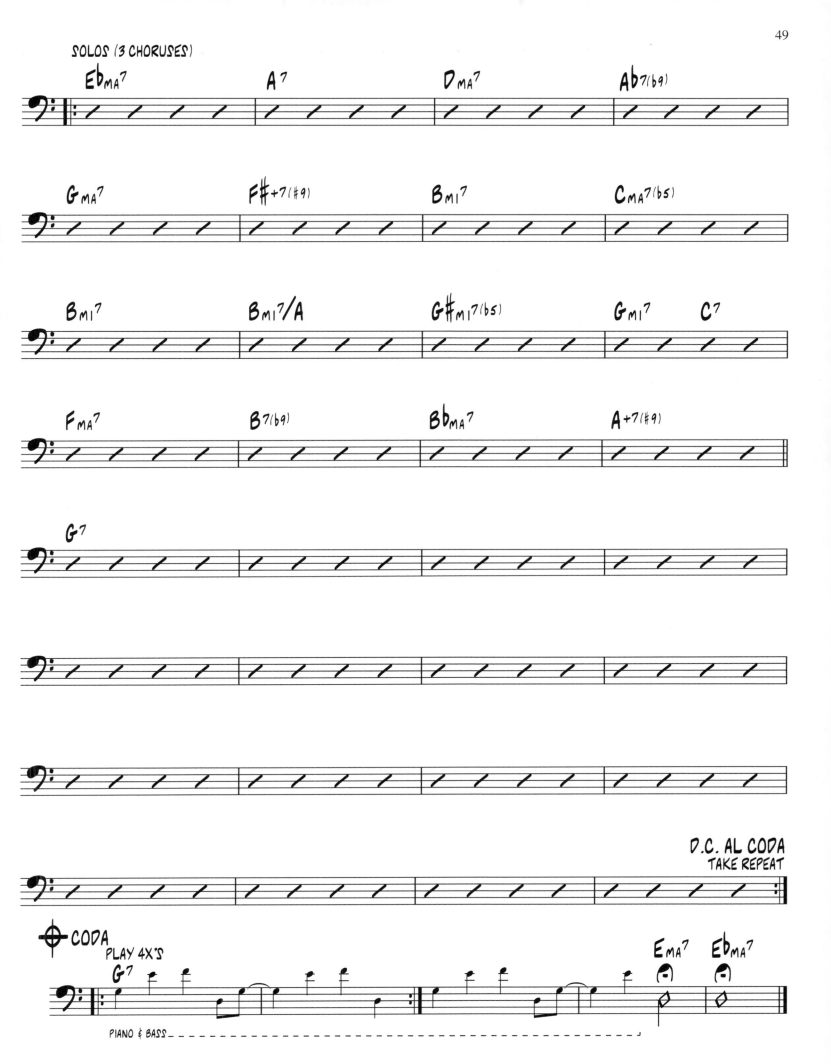

# CARAVAN

WORDS AND MUSIC BY DUKE ELLINGTON,
IRVING MILLS AND JUAN TIZOL

𝄢: C VERSION

Copyright © 1937 Sony/ATV Music Publishing LLC and EMI Mills Music Inc. in the U.S.A.
Copyright Renewed
This arrangement Copyright © 2015 Sony/ATV Music Publishing LLC and EMI Mills Music Inc. in the U.S.A.
All Rights on behalf of Sony/ATV Music Publishing LLC Administered by Sony/ATV Music Publishing LLC, 424 Church Street, Suite 1200, Nashville, TN 37219
All Rights for the world outside the U.S.A. Administered by EMI Mills Music Inc. (Publishing) and Alfred Music (Print)
International Copyright Secured   All Rights Reserved

# CONTEMPLATION

CD

9 : SPLIT TRACK/MELODY
10 : FULL STEREO TRACK

BY McCOY TYNER

: C VERSION

Copyright © 1963 Aisha Music
Copyright Renewed
This arrangement Copyright © 2015 Aisha Music
Administered by Prestige Music
International Copyright Secured   All Rights Reserved

# FREEDOM JAZZ DANCE

BY EDDIE HARRIS

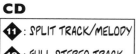

Copyright © 1965 Seventh House Ltd.
Copyright Renewed
This arrangement Copyright © 2015 Seventh House Ltd.
All Rights Reserved   Used by Permission

# IMPRESSIONS

BY JOHN COLTRANE

CD
13 : SPLIT TRACK/MELODY
14 : FULL STEREO TRACK

Copyright © 1974 (Renewed) JOWCOL MUSIC LLC
This arrangement Copyright © 2015 JOWCOL MUSIC LLC
International Copyright Secured   All Rights Reserved

# SHUTTERBUG

BY J.J. JOHNSON

CD
◆15: SPLIT TRACK/MELODY
◆16: FULL STEREO TRACK

𝄢: C VERSION

Copyright © 1960 TWO JAYS PUBLISHING CO.
Copyright Renewed
This arrangement Copyright © 2015 TWO JAYS PUBLISHING CO.
International Copyright Secured   All Rights Reserved

# SO WHAT

BY MILES DAVIS

Copyright © 1959 Jazz Horn Music Corporation
Copyright Renewed
This arrangement Copyright © 2002 Jazz Horn Music Corporation
All Rights Administered by Songs Of Kobalt Music Publishing
All Rights Reserved   Used by Permission

# YES OR NO

BY WAYNE SHORTER

Copyright © 1964 Miyako Music
Copyright Renewed
This arrangement Copyright © 2015 Miyako Music
All Rights Administered by Songs Of Kobalt Music Publishing
All Rights Reserved   Used by Permission

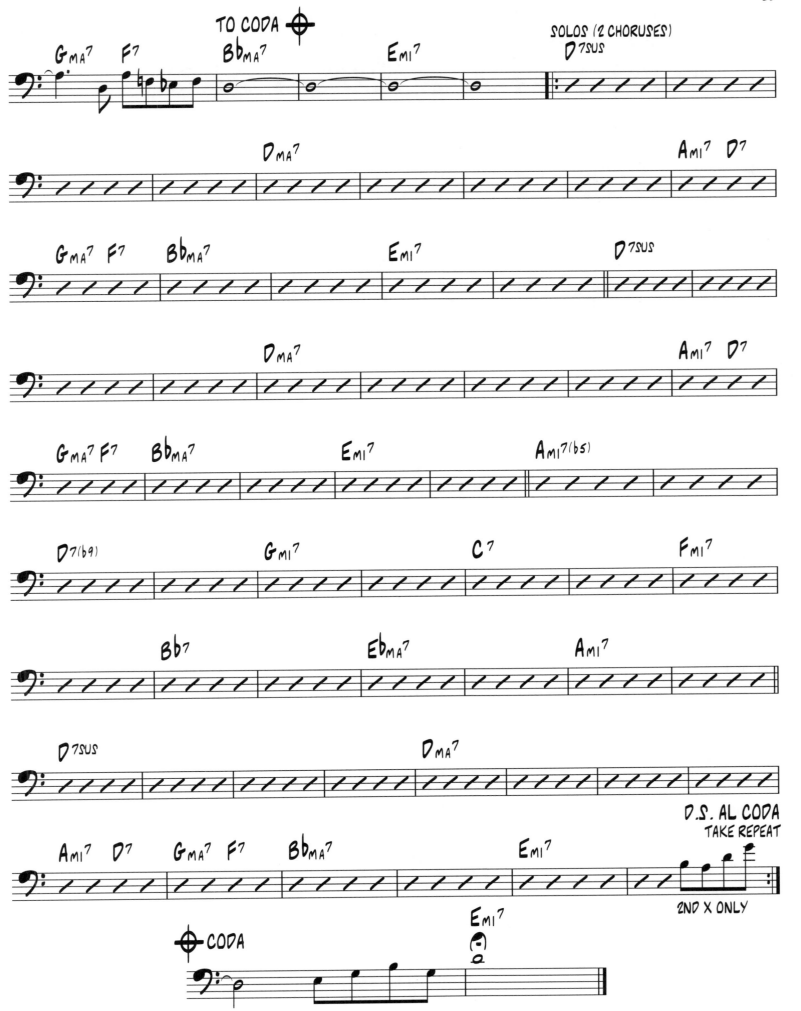

For use with all B-flat, E-flat, Bass Clef and C instruments, the Jazz Play-Along® Series is the ultimate learning tool for all jazz musicians. With musician-friendly lead sheets, melody cues, and other split-track choices on the included CD, these first-of-a-kind packages help you master improvisation while playing some of the greatest tunes of all time. FOR STUDY, each tune includes a split track with: melody cue with proper style and inflection • professional rhythm tracks • choruses for soloing • removable bass part • removable piano part. FOR PERFORMANCE, each tune also has: an additional full stereo accompaniment track (no melody) • additional choruses for soloing.

**1A. MAIDEN VOYAGE/ALL BLUES**
00843158 .............................. $16.99

**1. DUKE ELLINGTON**
00841644.............................. $16.99

**2. MILES DAVIS**
00841645.............................. $16.99

**3. THE BLUES**
00841646.............................. $16.99

**4. JAZZ BALLADS**
00841691.............................. $16.99

**5. BEST OF BEBOP**
00841689.............................. $16.99

**6. JAZZ CLASSICS WITH EASY CHANGES**
00841690.............................. $16.99

**7. ESSENTIAL JAZZ STANDARDS**
00843000.............................. $16.99

**8. ANTONIO CARLOS JOBIM AND THE ART OF THE BOSSA NOVA**
00843001.............................. $16.99

**9. DIZZY GILLESPIE**
00843002.............................. $16.99

**10. DISNEY CLASSICS**
00843003.............................. $16.99

**11. RODGERS AND HART FAVORITES**
00843004.............................. $16.99

**12. ESSENTIAL JAZZ CLASSICS**
00843005.............................. $16.99

**13. JOHN COLTRANE**
00843006.............................. $16.99

**14. IRVING BERLIN**
00843007.............................. $16.99

**15. RODGERS & HAMMERSTEIN**
00843008.............................. $16.99

**16. COLE PORTER**
00843009.............................. $16.99

**17. COUNT BASIE**
00843010.............................. $16.99

**18. HAROLD ARLEN**
00843011.............................. $16.99

**19. COOL JAZZ**
00843012.............................. $16.99

**20. CHRISTMAS CAROLS**
00843080.............................. $16.99

**21. RODGERS AND HART CLASSICS**
00843014.............................. $16.99

**22. WAYNE SHORTER**
00843015.............................. $16.99

**23. LATIN JAZZ**
00843016.............................. $16.99

**24. EARLY JAZZ STANDARDS**
00843017.............................. $16.99

**25. CHRISTMAS JAZZ**
00843018.............................. $16.99

**26. CHARLIE PARKER**
00843019.............................. $16.99

**27. GREAT JAZZ STANDARDS**
00843020.............................. $16.99

**28. BIG BAND ERA**
00843021.............................. $16.99

**29. LENNON AND MCCARTNEY**
00843022.............................. $16.99

**30. BLUES' BEST**
00843023.............................. $16.99

**31. JAZZ IN THREE**
00843024.............................. $16.99

**32. BEST OF SWING**
00843025.............................. $16.99

**33. SONNY ROLLINS**
00843029.............................. $16.99

**34. ALL TIME STANDARDS**
00843030.............................. $16.99

**35. BLUESY JAZZ**
00843031.............................. $16.99

**36. HORACE SILVER**
00843032.............................. $16.99

**37. BILL EVANS**
00843033.............................. $16.99

**38. YULETIDE JAZZ**
00843034.............................. $16.99

**39. "ALL THE THINGS YOU ARE" & MORE JEROME KERN SONGS**
00843035.............................. $16.99

**40. BOSSA NOVA**
00843036.............................. $16.99

**41. CLASSIC DUKE ELLINGTON**
00843037.............................. $16.99

**42. GERRY MULLIGAN FAVORITES**
00843038.............................. $16.99

**43. GERRY MULLIGAN CLASSICS**
00843039.............................. $16.99

**44. OLIVER NELSON**
00843040.............................. $16.99

**45. GEORGE GERSHWIN**
00103643.............................. $24.99

**46. BROADWAY JAZZ STANDARDS**
00843042.............................. $16.99

**47. CLASSIC JAZZ BALLADS**
00843043.............................. $16.99

**48. BEBOP CLASSICS**
00843044.............................. $16.99

**49. MILES DAVIS STANDARDS**
00843045.............................. $16.99

**50. GREAT JAZZ CLASSICS**
00843046.............................. $16.99

**51. UP-TEMPO JAZZ**
00843047.............................. $16.99

**52. STEVIE WONDER**
00843048.............................. $16.99

**53. RHYTHM CHANGES**
00843049.............................. $16.99

**54. "MOONLIGHT IN VERMONT" AND OTHER GREAT STANDARDS**
00843050.............................. $16.99

**55. BENNY GOLSON**
00843052.............................. $16.99

**56. "GEORGIA ON MY MIND" & OTHER SONGS BY HOAGY CARMICHAEL**
00843056.............................. $16.99

**57. VINCE GUARALDI**
00843057.............................. $16.99

**58. MORE LENNON AND MCCARTNEY**
00843059.............................. $16.99

**59. SOUL JAZZ**
00843060.............................. $16.99

**60. DEXTER GORDON**
00843061.............................. $16.99

**61. MONGO SANTAMARIA**
00843062.............................. $16.99

**62. JAZZ-ROCK FUSION**
00843063.............................. $16.99

**63. CLASSICAL JAZZ**
00843064.............................. $16.99

**64. TV TUNES**
00843065.............................. $16.99

**65. SMOOTH JAZZ**
00843066.............................. $16.99

**66. A CHARLIE BROWN CHRISTMAS**
00843067.............................. $16.99

**67. CHICK COREA**
00843068.............................. $16.99

**68. CHARLES MINGUS**
00843069.............................. $16.99

**69. CLASSIC JAZZ**
00843071.............................. $16.99

**71. COLE PORTER CLASSICS**
00843073.............................. $16.99

**72. CLASSIC JAZZ BALLADS**
00843074.............................. $16.99

**73. JAZZ/BLUES**
00843075.............................. $16.99

**74. BEST JAZZ CLASSICS**
00843076.............................. $16.99

**75. PAUL DESMOND**
00843077.............................. $16.99

**76. BROADWAY JAZZ BALLADS**
00843078.............................. $16.99

**78. STEELY DAN**
00843070..................$16.99

**79. MILES DAVIS CLASSICS**
00843081..................$16.99

**80. JIMI HENDRIX**
00843083..................$16.99

**81. FRANK SINATRA – CLASSICS**
00843084..................$16.99

**82. FRANK SINATRA – STANDARDS**
00843085..................$16.99

**83. ANDREW LLOYD WEBBER**
00843104..................$16.99

**84. BOSSA NOVA CLASSICS**
00843105..................$16.99

**85. MOTOWN HITS**
00843109..................$16.99

**86. BENNY GOODMAN**
00843110..................$16.99

**87. DIXIELAND**
00843111..................$16.99

**88. DUKE ELLINGTON FAVORITES**
00843112..................$16.99

**89. IRVING BERLIN FAVORITES**
00843113..................$16.99

**90. THELONIOUS MONK CLASSICS**
00841262..................$16.99

**91. THELONIOUS MONK FAVORITES**
00841263..................$16.99

**92. LEONARD BERNSTEIN**
00450134..................$16.99

**93. DISNEY FAVORITES**
00843142..................$16.99

**94. RAY**
00843143..................$16.99

**95. JAZZ AT THE LOUNGE**
00843144..................$16.99

**96. LATIN JAZZ STANDARDS**
00843145..................$16.99

**97. MAYBE I'M AMAZED***
00843148..................$16.99

**98. DAVE FRISHBERG**
00843149..................$16.99

**99. SWINGING STANDARDS**
00843150..................$16.99

**100. LOUIS ARMSTRONG**
00740423..................$16.99

**101. BUD POWELL**
00843152..................$16.99

**102. JAZZ POP**
00843153..................$16.99

**103. ON GREEN DOLPHIN STREET
& OTHER JAZZ CLASSICS**
00843154..................$16.99

**104. ELTON JOHN**
00843155..................$16.99

**105. SOULFUL JAZZ**
00843151..................$16.99

**106. SLO' JAZZ**
00843117..................$16.99

**107. MOTOWN CLASSICS**
00843116..................$16.99

**108. JAZZ WALTZ**
00843159..................$16.99

**109. OSCAR PETERSON**
00843160..................$16.99

**110. JUST STANDARDS**
00843161..................$16.99

**111. COOL CHRISTMAS**
00843162..................$16.99

**112. PAQUITO D'RIVERA – LATIN JAZZ***
48020662..................$16.99

**113. PAQUITO D'RIVERA – BRAZILIAN JAZZ***
48020663..................$19.99

**114. MODERN JAZZ QUARTET FAVORITES**
00843163..................$16.99

**115. THE SOUND OF MUSIC**
00843164..................$16.99

**116. JACO PASTORIUS**
00843165..................$16.99

**117. ANTONIO CARLOS JOBIM – MORE HITS**
00843166..................$16.99

**118. BIG JAZZ STANDARDS COLLECTION**
00843167..................$27.50

**119. JELLY ROLL MORTON**
00843168..................$16.99

**120. J.S. BACH**
00843169..................$16.99

**121. DJANGO REINHARDT**
00843170..................$16.99

**122. PAUL SIMON**
00843182..................$16.99

**123. BACHARACH & DAVID**
00843185..................$16.99

**124. JAZZ-ROCK HORN HITS**
00843186..................$16.99

**125. SAMMY NESTICO**
00843187..................$16.99

**126. COUNT BASIE CLASSICS**
00843157..................$16.99

**127. CHUCK MANGIONE**
00843188..................$16.99

**128. VOCAL STANDARDS (LOW VOICE)**
00843189..................$16.99

**129. VOCAL STANDARDS (HIGH VOICE)**
00843190..................$16.99

**130. VOCAL JAZZ (LOW VOICE)**
00843191..................$16.99

**131. VOCAL JAZZ (HIGH VOICE)**
00843192..................$16.99

**132. STAN GETZ ESSENTIALS**
00843193..................$16.99

**133. STAN GETZ FAVORITES**
00843194..................$16.99

**134. NURSERY RHYMES***
00843196..................$17.99

**135. JEFF BECK**
00843197..................$16.99

**136. NAT ADDERLEY**
00843198..................$16.99

**137. WES MONTGOMERY**
00843199..................$16.99

**138. FREDDIE HUBBARD**
00843200..................$16.99

**139. JULIAN "CANNONBALL" ADDERLEY**
00843201..................$16.99

**140. JOE ZAWINUL**
00843202..................$16.99

**141. BILL EVANS STANDARDS**
00843156..................$16.99

**142. CHARLIE PARKER GEMS**
00843222..................$16.99

**143. JUST THE BLUES**
00843223..................$16.99

**144. LEE MORGAN**
00843229..................$16.99

**145. COUNTRY STANDARDS**
00843230..................$16.99

**146. RAMSEY LEWIS**
00843231..................$16.99

**147. SAMBA**
00843232..................$16.99

**148. JOHN COLTRANE FAVORITES**
00843233..................$16.99

**149. JOHN COLTRANE – GIANT STEPS**
00843234..................$16.99

**150. JAZZ IMPROV BASICS**
00843195..................$19.99

**151. MODERN JAZZ QUARTET CLASSICS**
00843209..................$16.99

**152. J.J. JOHNSON**
00843210..................$16.99

**154. HENRY MANCINI**
00843213..................$16.99

**155. SMOOTH JAZZ CLASSICS**
00843215..................$16.99

**156. THELONIOUS MONK – EARLY GEMS**
00843216..................$16.99

**157. HYMNS**
00843217..................$16.99

**158. JAZZ COVERS ROCK**
00843219..................$16.99

**159. MOZART**
00843220..................$16.99

**160. GEORGE SHEARING**
14041531..................$16.99

**161. DAVE BRUBECK**
14041556..................$16.99

**162. BIG CHRISTMAS COLLECTION**
00843221..................$24.99

**163. JOHN COLTRANE STANDARDS**
00843235..................$16.99

**164. HERB ALPERT**
14041775..................$16.99

**165. GEORGE BENSON**
00843240..................$16.99

**166. ORNETTE COLEMAN**
00843241..................$16.99

**167. JOHNNY MANDEL**
00103642..................$16.99

**168. TADD DAMERON**
00103663..................$16.99

**169. BEST JAZZ STANDARDS**
00109249..................$19.99

**170. ULTIMATE JAZZ STANDARDS**
00109250..................$19.99

**171. RADIOHEAD**
00109305..................$16.99

**172. POP STANDARDS**
00111669..................$16.99

**174. TIN PAN ALLEY**
00119125..................$16.99

**175. TANGO**
00119836..................$16.99

**176. JOHNNY MERCER**
00119838..................$16.99

**177. THE II-V-I PROGRESSION**
00843239..................$19.99

**181. BILLY JOEL**
00122329..................$16.99

**182. "RHAPSODY IN BLUE" & 7 OTHER
CLASSICAL-BASED JAZZ PIECES**
00116847..................$16.99

**183. SONDHEIM**
00126253..................$16.99

**187. CHRISTMAS FAVORITES**
00128393..................$16.99

Prices, contents, and availability subject to change without notice.

7777 W. BLUEMOUND RD. P.O. BOX 13819 MILWAUKEE, WI 53213

For complete songlists and more visit
**halleonard.com**

*These CDs do not include split tracks.

# The Best-Selling Jazz Book of All Time Is Now Legal!

The Real Books are the most popular jazz books of all time. Since the 1970s, musicians have trusted these volumes to get them through every gig, night after night. The problem is that the books were illegally produced and distributed, without any regard to copyright law, or royalties paid to the composers who created these musical masterpieces.

Hal Leonard is very proud to present the first legitimate and legal editions of these books ever produced. You won't even notice the difference, other than all the notorious errors being fixed: the covers and typeface look the same, the song lists are nearly identical, and the price for our edition is even cheaper than the originals!

Every conscientious musician will appreciate that these books are now produced accurately and ethically, benefitting the songwriters that we owe for some of the greatest tunes of all time!

*Also available:*

| | | |
|---|---|---|
| 00240264 | The Real Blues Book | $34.99 |
| 00310910 | The Real Bluegrass Book | $29.99 |
| 00240440 | The Trane Book | $22.99 |
| 00240137 | Miles Davis Real Book | $19.95 |
| 00240355 | The Real Dixieland Book | $29.99 |
| 00122335 | The Real Dixieland Book B♭ Edition | $29.99 |
| 00240235 | The Duke Ellington Real Book | $19.99 |
| 00240268 | The Real Jazz Solos Book | $30.00 |
| 00240348 | The Real Latin Book | $35.00 |
| 00127107 | The Real Latin Book B♭ Edition | $35.00 |
| 00240358 | The Charlie Parker Real Book | $19.99 |
| 00240331 | The Bud Powell Real Book | $19.99 |
| 00240437 | The Real R&B Book | $39.99 |
| 00240313 | The Real Rock Book | $35.00 |
| 00240323 | The Real Rock Book – Vol. 2 | $35.00 |
| 00240359 | The Real Tab Book | $32.50 |
| 00240317 | The Real Worship Book | $29.99 |

## VOLUME 1

| | | |
|---|---|---|
| 00240221 | C Edition | $35.00 |
| 00240224 | B♭ Edition | $35.00 |
| 00240225 | E♭ Edition | $35.00 |
| 00240226 | Bass Clef Edition | $35.00 |
| 00240292 | C Edition 6 x 9 | $30.00 |
| 00240339 | B♭ Edition 6 x 9 | $30.00 |
| 00451087 | C Edition on CD-ROM | $25.00 |
| 00240302 | A-D CD Backing Tracks | $24.99 |
| 00240303 | E-J CD Backing Tracks | $24.95 |
| 00240304 | L-R CD Backing Tracks | $24.95 |
| 00240305 | S-Z CD Backing Tracks | $24.99 |
| 00110604 | Book/USB Flash Drive Backing Tracks Pack | $79.99 |
| 00110599 | USB Flash Drive Only | $50.00 |

## VOLUME 2

| | | |
|---|---|---|
| 00240222 | C Edition | $35.50 |
| 00240227 | B♭ Edition | $35.00 |
| 00240228 | E♭ Edition | $35.00 |
| 00240229 | Bass Clef Edition | $35.00 |
| 00240293 | C Edition 6 x 9 | $30.00 |
| 00125900 | B♭ Edition 6 x 9 | $30.00 |
| 00451088 | C Edition on CD-ROM | $27.99 |
| 00240351 | A-D CD Backing Tracks | $24.99 |
| 00240352 | E-I CD Backing Tracks | $24.99 |
| 00240353 | J-R CD Backing Tracks | $24.99 |
| 00240354 | S-Z CD Backing Tracks | $24.99 |

## VOLUME 3

| | | |
|---|---|---|
| 00240233 | C Edition | $35.00 |
| 00240284 | B♭ Edition | $35.00 |
| 00240285 | E♭ Edition | $35.00 |
| 00240286 | Bass Clef Edition | $35.00 |
| 00240338 | C Edition 6 x 9 | $30.00 |
| 00451089 | C Edition on CD-ROM | $29.99 |

## VOLUME 4

| | | |
|---|---|---|
| 00240296 | C Edition | $35.00 |
| 00103348 | B♭ Edition | $35.00 |
| 00103349 | E♭ Edition | $35.00 |
| 00103350 | Bass Clef Edition | $35.00 |

## VOLUME 5

| | | |
|---|---|---|
| 00240349 | C Edition | $35.00 |

## THE REAL CHRISTMAS BOOK

| | | |
|---|---|---|
| 00240306 | C Edition | $29.99 |
| 00240345 | B♭ Edition | $29.99 |
| 00240346 | E♭ Edition | $29.99 |
| 00240347 | Bass Clef Edition | $29.99 |
| 00240431 | A-G CD Backing Tracks | $24.99 |
| 00240432 | H-M CD Backing Tracks | $24.99 |
| 00240433 | N-Y CD Backing Tracks | $24.99 |

## THE REAL VOCAL BOOK

| | | |
|---|---|---|
| 00240230 | Volume 1 High Voice | $35.00 |
| 00240307 | Volume 1 Low Voice | $35.00 |
| 00240231 | Volume 2 High Voice | $35.00 |
| 00240308 | Volume 2 Low Voice | $35.00 |
| 00240391 | Volume 3 High Voice | $35.00 |
| 00240392 | Volume 3 Low Voice | $35.00 |
| 00118318 | Volume 4 High Voice | $35.00 |
| 00118319 | Volume 4 Low Voice | $35.00 |

## THE REAL BOOK – STAFF PAPER

| | | |
|---|---|---|
| 00240327 | | $10.99 |

## HOW TO PLAY FROM A REAL BOOK

For All Musicians
*by Robert Rawlins*

| | | |
|---|---|---|
| 00312097 | | $17.50 |

**Complete song lists online at www.halleonard.com**
*Prices, content, and availability subject to change without notice.*

7777 W. Bluemound Rd. P.O. Box 13819 Milwaukee, WI 53213

1214

# ARTIST TRANSCRIPTIONS

**Artist Transcriptions** are authentic, note-for-note transcriptions of today's hottest artists in jazz, pop and rock. These outstanding, accurate arrangements are in an easy-to-read format which includes all essential lines. **Artist Transcriptions** can be used to perform, sequence or for reference.

## CLARINET
| | | |
|---|---|---|
| 00672423 | Buddy De Franco Collection | $19.95 |

## FLUTE
| | | |
|---|---|---|
| 00672379 | Eric Dolphy Collection | $19.95 |
| 00672582 | The Very Best of James Galway | $16.99 |
| 00672372 | James Moody Collection – Sax and Flute | $19.95 |

## GUITAR & BASS
| | | |
|---|---|---|
| 00660113 | The Guitar Style of George Benson | $14.95 |
| 00699072 | Guitar Book of Pierre Bensusan | $29.95 |
| 00672331 | Ron Carter – Acoustic Bass | $16.95 |
| 00672307 | Stanley Clarke Collection | $19.95 |
| 00660115 | Al Di Meola – Friday Night in San Francisco | $14.95 |
| 00604043 | Al Di Meola – Music, Words, Pictures | $14.95 |
| 00672574 | Al Di Meola – Pursuit of Radical Rhapsody | $22.99 |
| 00673245 | Jazz Style of Tal Farlow | $19.95 |
| 00699306 | Jim Hall – Exploring Jazz Guitar | $19.95 |
| 00604049 | Allan Holdsworth – Reaching for the Uncommon Chord | $14.95 |
| 00699215 | Leo Kottke – Eight Songs | $14.95 |
| 00675536 | Wes Montgomery – Guitar Transcriptions | $17.95 |
| 00672353 | Joe Pass Collection | $18.95 |
| 00673216 | John Patitucci | $16.95 |
| 00027083 | Django Reinhardt Anthology | $14.95 |
| 00026711 | Genius of Django Reinhardt | $10.95 |
| 00672374 | Johnny Smith Guitar Solos | $19.99 |

## PIANO & KEYBOARD
| | | |
|---|---|---|
| 00672338 | Monty Alexander Collection | $19.95 |
| 00672487 | Monty Alexander Plays Standards | $19.95 |
| 00672520 | Count Basie Collection | $19.95 |
| 00672439 | Cyrus Chestnut Collection | $19.95 |
| 00672300 | Chick Corea – Paint the World | $12.95 |
| 14037739 | Storyville Presents Duke Ellington | $19.99 |
| 00672537 | Bill Evans at Town Hall | $16.95 |
| 00672548 | The Mastery of Bill Evans | $12.95 |
| 00672425 | Bill Evans – Piano Interpretations | $19.95 |
| 00672365 | Bill Evans – Piano Standards | $19.95 |
| 00672510 | Bill Evans Trio – Vol. 1: 1959-1961 | $24.95 |
| 00672511 | Bill Evans Trio – Vol. 2: 1962-1965 | $24.95 |
| 00672512 | Bill Evans Trio – Vol. 3: 1968-1974 | $24.95 |
| 00672513 | Bill Evans Trio – Vol. 4: 1979-1980 | $24.95 |
| 00672381 | Tommy Flanagan Collection | $24.99 |
| 00672492 | Benny Goodman Collection | $16.95 |
| 00672486 | Vince Guaraldi Collection | $19.95 |
| 00672419 | Herbie Hancock Collection | $19.95 |
| 00672438 | Hampton Hawes | $19.95 |
| 14037738 | Storyville Presents Earl Hines | $19.99 |
| 00672322 | Ahmad Jamal Collection | $22.95 |
| 00672564 | Best of Jeff Lorber | $17.99 |
| 00672476 | Brad Mehldau Collection | $19.99 |
| 00672388 | Best of Thelonious Monk | $19.95 |
| 00672389 | Thelonious Monk Collection | $19.95 |

| | | |
|---|---|---|
| 00672390 | Thelonious Monk Plays Jazz Standards – Volume 1 | $19.95 |
| 00672391 | Thelonious Monk Plays Jazz Standards – Volume 2 | $19.95 |
| 00672433 | Jelly Roll Morton – The Piano Rolls | $12.95 |
| 00672553 | Charlie Parker for Piano | $19.95 |
| 00672542 | Oscar Peterson – Jazz Piano Solos | $16.95 |
| 00672562 | Oscar Peterson – A Jazz Portrait of Frank Sinatra | $19.95 |
| 00672544 | Oscar Peterson – Originals | $9.95 |
| 00672532 | Oscar Peterson – Plays Broadway | $19.95 |
| 00672531 | Oscar Peterson – Plays Duke Ellington | $19.95 |
| 00672563 | Oscar Peterson – A Royal Wedding Suite | $19.99 |
| 00672533 | Oscar Peterson – Trios | $24.95 |
| 00672543 | Oscar Peterson Trio – Canadiana Suite | $10.99 |
| 00672534 | Very Best of Oscar Peterson | $22.95 |
| 00672371 | Bud Powell Classics | $19.95 |
| 00672376 | Bud Powell Collection | $19.95 |
| 00672507 | Gonzalo Rubalcaba Collection | $19.95 |
| 00672303 | Horace Silver Collection | $19.95 |
| 00672316 | Art Tatum Collection | $22.95 |
| 00672355 | Art Tatum Solo Book | $19.95 |
| 00672357 | Billy Taylor Collection | $24.95 |
| 00673215 | McCoy Tyner | $16.95 |
| 00672321 | Cedar Walton Collection | $19.95 |
| 00672519 | Kenny Werner Collection | $19.95 |
| 00672434 | Teddy Wilson Collection | $19.95 |
| 14037740 | Storyville Presents Teddy Wilson | $19.99 |

## SAXOPHONE
| | | |
|---|---|---|
| 00672566 | The Mindi Abair Collection | $14.99 |
| 00673244 | Julian "Cannonball" Adderley Collection | $19.95 |
| 00673237 | Michael Brecker | $19.95 |
| 00672429 | Michael Brecker Collection | $19.95 |
| 00672315 | Benny Carter Plays Standards | $22.95 |
| 00672394 | James Carter Collection | $19.95 |
| 00672349 | John Coltrane Plays Giant Steps | $19.95 |
| 00672529 | John Coltrane – Giant Steps | $14.99 |
| 00672494 | John Coltrane – A Love Supreme | $14.95 |
| 00307393 | John Coltrane – Omnibook: C Instruments | $24.99 |
| 00307391 | John Coltrane – Omnibook: B-flat Instruments | $19.99 |
| 00307392 | John Coltrane – Omnibook: E-flat Instruments | $24.99 |
| 00307394 | John Coltrane – Omnibook: Bass Clef Instruments | $24.99 |
| 00672493 | John Coltrane Plays "Coltrane Changes" | $19.95 |
| 00672453 | John Coltrane Plays Standards | $19.95 |
| 00673233 | John Coltrane Solos | $22.95 |
| 00672328 | Paul Desmond Collection | $19.95 |
| 00672379 | Eric Dolphy Collection | $19.95 |
| 00672530 | Kenny Garrett Collection | $19.95 |
| 00699375 | Stan Getz | $19.95 |

| | | |
|---|---|---|
| 00672377 | Stan Getz – Bossa Novas | $19.95 |
| 00672375 | Stan Getz – Standards | $18.95 |
| 00673254 | Great Tenor Sax Solos | $18.95 |
| 00672523 | Coleman Hawkins Collection | $19.95 |
| 00673252 | Joe Henderson – Selections from "Lush Life" & "So Near So Far" | $19.95 |
| 00672330 | Best of Joe Henderson | $22.95 |
| 00672350 | Tenor Saxophone Standards | $18.95 |
| 00673239 | Best of Kenny G | $19.95 |
| 00673229 | Kenny G – Breathless | $19.95 |
| 00672462 | Kenny G – Classics in the Key of G | $19.95 |
| 00672485 | Kenny G – Faith: A Holiday Album | $14.95 |
| 00672373 | Kenny G – The Moment | $19.95 |
| 00672326 | Joe Lovano Collection | $19.95 |
| 00672498 | Jackie McLean Collection | $19.95 |
| 00672372 | James Moody Collection – Sax and Flute | $19.95 |
| 00672416 | Frank Morgan Collection | $19.95 |
| 00672539 | Gerry Mulligan Collection | $19.95 |
| 00672352 | Charlie Parker Collection | $19.95 |
| 00672561 | Best of Sonny Rollins | $19.95 |
| 00672444 | Sonny Rollins Collection | $19.95 |
| 00102751 | Sonny Rollins with the Modern Jazz Quartet | $17.99 |
| 00675000 | David Sanborn Collection | $17.95 |
| 00672528 | Bud Shank Collection | $19.95 |
| 00672491 | New Best of Wayne Shorter | $19.95 |
| 00672550 | The Sonny Stitt Collection | $19.95 |
| 00672350 | Tenor Saxophone Standards | $18.95 |
| 00672567 | The Best of Kim Waters | $17.99 |
| 00672524 | Lester Young Collection | $19.95 |

## TROMBONE
| | | |
|---|---|---|
| 00672332 | J.J. Johnson Collection | $19.95 |
| 00672489 | Steve Turré Collection | $19.99 |

## TRUMPET
| | | |
|---|---|---|
| 00672557 | Herb Alpert Collection | $14.99 |
| 00672480 | Louis Armstrong Collection | $17.95 |
| 00672481 | Louis Armstrong Plays Standards | $17.95 |
| 00672435 | Chet Baker Collection | $19.95 |
| 00672556 | Best of Chris Botti | $19.95 |
| 00672448 | Miles Davis – Originals, Vol. 1 | $19.95 |
| 00672451 | Miles Davis – Originals, Vol. 2 | $19.95 |
| 00672450 | Miles Davis – Standards, Vol. 1 | $19.95 |
| 00672449 | Miles Davis – Standards, Vol. 2 | $19.95 |
| 00672479 | Dizzy Gillespie Collection | $19.95 |
| 00673214 | Freddie Hubbard | $14.95 |
| 00672382 | Tom Harrell – Jazz Trumpet | $19.95 |
| 00672363 | Jazz Trumpet Solos | $9.95 |
| 00672506 | Chuck Mangione Collection | $19.95 |
| 00672525 | Arturo Sandoval – Trumpet Evolution | $19.95 |

**HAL•LEONARD®**
**CORPORATION**
7777 W. BLUEMOUND RD. P.O. BOX 13819 MILWAUKEE, WI 53213

Visit our web site for a complete listing of our titles with songlists at

**www.halleonard.com**

Prices and availability subject to change without notice.

0913

# *Jazz Instruction & Improvisation*

## BOOKS FOR ALL INSTRUMENTS FROM HAL LEONARD

### AN APPROACH TO JAZZ IMPROVISATION
*by Dave Pozzi*
*Musicians Institute Press*
Explore the styles of Charlie Parker, Sonny Rollins, Bud Powell and others with this comprehensive guide to jazz improvisation. Covers: scale choices • chord analysis • phrasing • melodies • harmonic progressions • more.
00695135  Book/CD Pack......................................$17.95

### THE ART OF MODULATING
FOR PIANISTS AND JAZZ MUSICIANS
*by Carlos Salzedo &*
*Lucile Lawrence*
*Schirmer*
*The Art of Modulating* is a treatise originally intended for the harp, but this edition has been edited for use by intermediate keyboardists and other musicians who have an understanding of basic music theory. In its pages you will find: table of intervals; modulation rules; modulation formulas; examples of modulation; extensions and cadences; ten fragments of dances; five characteristic pieces; and more.
50490581  .......................................................$19.99

### BUILDING A JAZZ VOCABULARY
*By Mike Steinel*
A valuable resource for learning the basics of jazz from Mike Steinel of the University of North Texas. It covers: the basics of jazz • how to build effective solos • a comprehensive practice routine • and a jazz vocabulary of the masters.
00849911  .......................................................$19.95

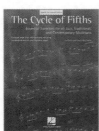

### THE CYCLE OF FIFTHS
*by Emile and Laura De Cosmo*
This essential instruction book provides more than 450 exercises, including hundreds of melodic and rhythmic ideas. The book is designed to help improvisors master the cycle of fifths, one of the primary progressions in music. Guaranteed to refine technique, enhance improvisational fluency, and improve sight-reading!
00311114  .......................................................$16.99

### THE DIATONIC CYCLE
*by Emile and Laura De Cosmo*
Renowned jazz educators Emile and Laura De Cosmo provide more than 300 exercises to help improvisors tackle one of music's most common progressions: the diatonic cycle. This book is guaranteed to refine technique, enhance improvisational fluency, and improve sight-reading!
00311115  .......................................................$16.95

### EAR TRAINING
*by Keith Wyatt,*
*Carl Schroeder and Joe Elliott*
*Musicians Institute Press*
Covers: basic pitch matching • singing major and minor scales • identifying intervals • transcribing melodies and rhythm • identifying chords and progressions • seventh chords and the blues • modal interchange, chromaticism, modulation • and more.
00695198  Book/2-CD Pack ...................................$24.95

### EXERCISES AND ETUDES FOR THE JAZZ INSTRUMENTALIST
*by J.J. Johnson*
Designed as study material and playable by any instrument, these pieces run the gamut of the jazz experience, featuring common and uncommon time signatures and keys, and styles from ballads to funk. They are progressively graded so that both beginners and professionals will be challenged by the demands of this wonderful music.
00842018  Bass Clef Edition ..................................$16.95
00842042  Treble Clef Edition ...............................$16.95

### JAZZOLOGY
THE ENCYCLOPEDIA OF JAZZ THEORY FOR ALL MUSICIANS
*by Robert Rawlins and*
*Nor Eddine Bahha*
This comprehensive resource covers a variety of jazz topics, for beginners and pros of any instrument. The book serves as an encyclopedia for reference, a thorough methodology for the student, and a workbook for the classroom.
00311167  ........................................................$19.99

### JAZZ THEORY RESOURCES
*by Bert Ligon*
*Houston Publishing, Inc.*
This is a jazz theory text in two volumes. **Volume 1 includes**: review of basic theory • rhythm in jazz performance • triadic generalization • diatonic harmonic progressions and analysis • substitutions and turnarounds • and more. **Volume 2 includes**: modes and modal frameworks • quartal harmony • extended tertian structures and triadic superimposition • pentatonic applications • coloring "outside" the lines and beyond • and more.
00030458  Volume 1 .............................................$39.95
00030459  Volume 2 .............................................$29.95

### JOY OF IMPROV
*by Dave Frank*
*and John Amaral*
This book/CD course on improvisation for all instruments and all styles will help players develop monster musical skills! Book One imparts a solid basis in technique, rhythm, chord theory, ear training and improv concepts. **Book Two** explores more advanced chord voicings, chord arranging techniques and more challenging blues and melodic lines. The CD can be used as a listening and play-along tool.
00220005  Book 1 – Book/CD Pack......................$27.99
00220006  Book 2 – Book/CD Pack......................$26.99

### THE PATH TO JAZZ IMPROVISATION
*by Emile and Laura De Cosmo*
This fascinating jazz instruction book offers an innovative, scholarly approach to the art of improvisation. It includes in-depth analysis and lessons about: cycle of fifths • diatonic cycle • overtone series • pentatonic scale • harmonic and melodic minor scale • polytonal order of keys • blues and bebop scales • modes • and more.
00310904  .......................................................$14.99

### THE SOURCE
THE DICTIONARY OF CONTEMPORARY AND TRADITIONAL SCALES
*by Steve Barta*
This book serves as an informative guide for people who are looking for good, solid information regarding scales, chords, and how they work together. It provides right and left hand fingerings for scales, chords, and complete inversions. Includes over 20 different scales, each written in all 12 keys.
00240885  .......................................................$18.99

### 21 BEBOP EXERCISES
*by Steve Rawlins*
This book/CD pack is both a warm-up collection and a manual for bebop phrasing. Its tasty and sophisticated exercises will help you develop your proficiency with jazz interpretation. It concentrates on practice in all twelve keys — moving higher by half-step — to help develop dexterity and range. The companion CD includes all of the exercises in 12 keys.
00315341  Book/CD Pack......................................$17.95

## HAL•LEONARD® CORPORATION
7777 W. BLUEMOUND RD. P.O. BOX 13819 MILWAUKEE, WI 53213

Visit Hal Leonard online at
**www.halleonard.com**

Prices, contents & availability
subject to change without notice.

0113